KINGFISHER EXPLORER BOOKS

THE AGE OF
STEAM

Jonathan Rutland

Designed by David Nash

Illustrators
Mike Atkinson · Gordon Davies · Ron Jobson
Mike Kelly · Bernard Robinson · Mike Trim

KINGFISHER BOOKS

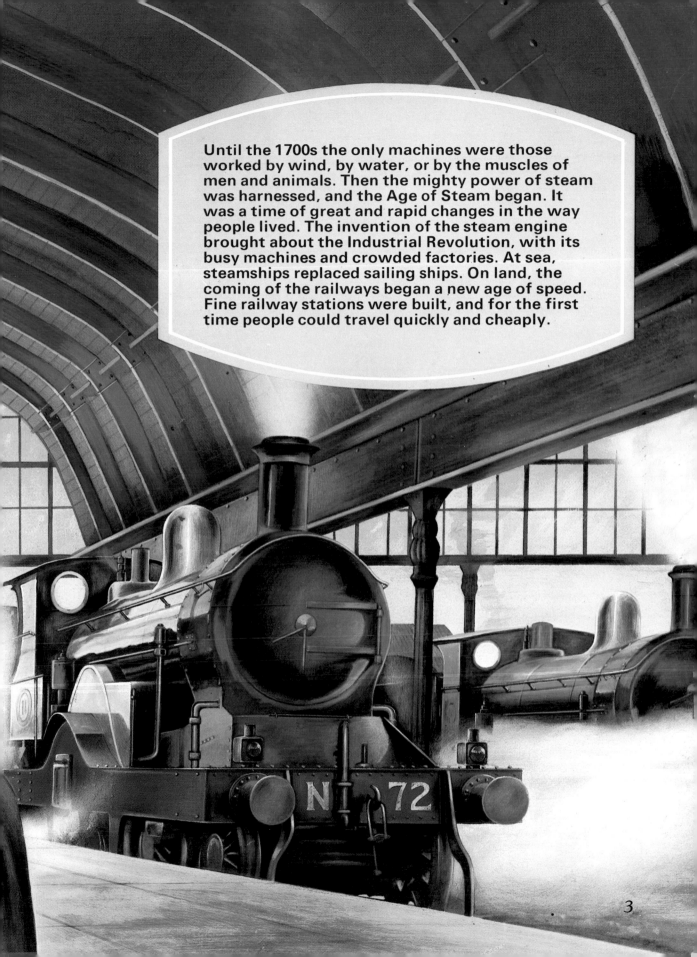

Until the 1700s the only machines were those worked by wind, by water, or by the muscles of men and animals. Then the mighty power of steam was harnessed, and the Age of Steam began. It was a time of great and rapid changes in the way people lived. The invention of the steam engine brought about the Industrial Revolution, with its busy machines and crowded factories. At sea, steamships replaced sailing ships. On land, the coming of the railways began a new age of speed. Fine railway stations were built, and for the first time people could travel quickly and cheaply.

The Steam Engine

Since ancient times men have known the power of steam. The Greeks wondered how steam power could be used. But they never got further than making toys, such as spinning balls driven by tiny jets of steam.

The great step forward came in England in the 1700s. The Cornish tin miners and the coal miners of Newcastle worked deep underground. The mines were dark and dangerous. To protect them from flooding, the miners needed powerful pumps. It was to drive these pumps that the first steam engines were invented. One of the most successful was invented by Thomas Newcomen in 1712.

In Newcomen's engine coal heated water in the boiler to make steam. The steam was let into a cylinder and forced a piston up. Then the steam was cooled, or condensed, by a spray of water. As it cooled, a vacuum was created inside the cylinder. The vacuum sucked the piston down again. Then more steam was let in and the next stroke of the engine began.

The piston was joined to a 'rocking beam' on top of the engine. As the piston moved one end of the rocking beam up and down, the other end worked a pump at the bottom of the mine. Newcomen's engine was slow and noisy, but the miners were thankful for it. Soon more were built, with improvements to make them pump faster. The diagram opposite shows an improved Newcomen engine. It was built by James Watt, a Scottish

WATT'S
PUMPING
ENGINE

rocking
beam

pump
rod

piston

cylinder

steam

cold
water

condenser

rocking beam

James Watt improved the steam engine by adding a separate condenser, an air pump and a 'steam jacket' to keep the cylinder hot. His 'rotary engine' could turn wheels, and wheels could be used to drive machines in mills and factories.

main wheel

'planet'

'sun'

instrument maker. Watt realized that a lot of energy was wasted heating and cooling the steam in the same cylinder. So he cooled the steam in a separate compartment, called a *condenser*.

Steam Turns Wheels

So far, steam could only push a rocking beam up and down, like a seesaw. This was fine for working a pump, but of little use for anything else. Steam power could not turn wheels smoothly until Watt made use of 'sun and planet' wheels in his rotary engine of 1782.

Instead of working a pump, the rocking beam was connected by a rod to a big wheel. The 'sun' was a small toothed wheel fixed to the centre of the big wheel. The 'planet' was a similar small wheel on the end of the connecting rod. As the rod moved up and down, the 'planet' travelled round the 'sun', and turned the big wheel.

Watt also increased his engine's power by using steam to drive the piston up *and* down. This was the first 'double action' steam engine.

The new engines changed people's lives. Before, most people lived in villages. They worked on farms, or in small workshops, or at home. They spun cotton into thread on little spinning wheels, and wove the thread into cloth on small looms.

Now, one steam engine could drive rows of big looms, by means of belts connected to its wheel. Factories and mills were built in the towns to house the new machines, which could work quickly and cheaply. Country folk had to leave their homes and move to the towns to work in the factories.

fire-engine with steam-driven pump

STEAM FIRSTS
1698 Thomas Savery builds the first steam-driven pump.
1712 Thomas Newcomen invents the beam-engine.
1769 Nicholas Cugnot builds the first steam-driven vehicle—a gun carriage.
1780s James Watt builds the first 'double action' steam engine.
1787 John Fitch builds the first practical steamboat.
1804 Richard Trevithick builds the first steam locomotive.

Nasmyth's steam hammer
after a painting
by the inventor

Steam at Work

Steam was put to work in many different ways. In fact steam engines did many of the jobs that petrol engines and electric motors do today.

In factories and workshops steam was used to drive powerful machines. With the coming of the machine age, metal-working became an important industry. In the iron foundries huge steam hammers were used to pound the red-hot metal into shape. Invented by James Nasmyth in 1842, the steam hammer was used to make parts for the new steam ships. It was worked by a double action steam engine. As steam entered the cylinder, the piston raised the hammer. Then more steam was forced in above the piston, sending the hammer crashing down.

For some time, though, steam and horses worked side by side. For example, fire engines were still pulled through the streets by horses. But steam engines worked the pumps.

On the farm steam engines drove saws and threshing machines. But the first engines were too heavy to move. A better idea was the traction engine, which was like a railway locomotive but could travel along the roads or across fields. Traction engines were slow but very powerful. They pulled carts and drove the roundabouts at travelling fairs.

Steam on Rails

In 1804 Richard Trevithick, an English mining engineer, built the first steam 'locomotive'. It could move on rails under its own steam, pulling a train of wagons. Trevithick's locomotive proved that steam power could replace horses. Soon other steam locomotives were built to haul coal wagons from the mines. One of the best known was called *Puffing Billy*.

People were fascinated by these puffing mechanical monsters. But most were too frightened to ride on one. At that time no one had ever travelled faster than a horse could gallop. Doctors warned that railway passengers would probably die of shock!

Pioneers like George Stephenson and his son Robert made rail travel successful. Their locomotives, such as *Locomotion* and *Rocket*, were better than any others. In 1825 Stephenson loco-motives were chosen to pull wagons on the new Stockton and Darlington Railway.

This was the first public steam railway in the world. On the first run, crowds flocked to see the train. A man on horseback rode in front with a red flag to make sure everyone kept well clear. But before the locomotive set off, it let out a loud hiss of steam, terrifying the people and making the horse rear in panic. The railway age had begun!

The Golden Age of Railways

Soon railways were being built all over Britain and in other countries. The Stephensons' dream had come true: everyone travelled by train. True, the first passengers rode in uncomfortable open wagons. At first, rich people preferred to sit in their own coaches loaded on to flat wagons, while the horses travelled in a special horse box.

Before long the railways were competing fiercely against one another. Passengers wanted greater comfort and more speed. There were even races between rival trains.

Steam ruled the railways for 100 years. Locomotives grew bigger and more powerful, with bigger boilers and more driving wheels. The fastest steam locomotive of all, *Mallard*, reached a speed of over 200 kilometres per hour in 1938. Its smooth, streamlined shape was very different from that of *Rocket*. Yet its workings were basically the same.

Mallard

Mallet

Big Boy

Railway record-breakers: the world's fastest steam locomotive, the *Mallard*, reached a speed of 203 km/h in 1938; the most powerful, an American *Mallet,* hauled goods trains two kilometres long; and the largest, the Union Pacific *Big Boy,* weighed over 500 tonnes with its tender.

a splendid drawing-room carriage of the 1800s

A powerful New Zealand locomotive of the 1930's. For 100 years steam locomotives hauled passengers and freight throughout the world.

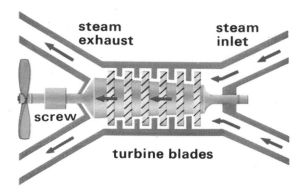

How a steam turbine works. Steam from the boiler flows through pipes at great speed. The jets of steam hit the blades of the turbine, spinning them round. This is a marine turbine, driving a ship's screw.

The Power of Steam

The mighty power of steam could be used to drive turbines to make electricity, to drive ships' engines, and of course to drive railway locomotives. In fact, the steam locomotive was most people's idea of what a steam engine looked and sounded like.

The steam locomotive was a powerhouse on wheels. It could pull heavy loads at low speeds or lighter loads at high speeds. Every locomotive had a boiler made of many tubes running from end to end. Coal for the fire and water for the boiler were carried in a tender behind the locomotive.

While the engine driver controlled the train, the fireman shovelled coal into the fire-box. The flames and heat were sucked through the boiler tubes, heating the water and changing it to steam.

As steam was let into the cylinders, the pistons drove backwards and forwards. Each piston was fixed to a connecting rod linked to a crank on the big driving wheels. The used steam escaped through a blast-pipe and up the chimney. This made a puffing noise and created a draught for the fire, so that more heat was sucked into the boiler. Extra water could be scooped up at speed from troughs between the rails. Some locomotives used wood or oil instead of coal.

A few steam locomotives are still at work. But diesel and electric trains (which are cleaner and cheaper to run) have replaced most of them.

firebox

Steamships

At first, inventors did not have much success trying to put steam engines into boats. Sails and oars had been used for so long that it was difficult to work out how to make an engine drive a boat through the water.

An American called Robert Fulton came up with the answer. He tried using water jets and mechanical paddles. Finally he fitted a boat with paddle wheels, turned by a single-cylinder engine. This boat, the *Clermont*, worked well and began carrying passengers in 1807.

Before long, bigger and better steamers appeared. Some, like the Mississippi steamboats, had paddle wheels at the stern. Others had a paddle wheel on either side. At first no one thought a steamboat would be safe in the open sea. What would happen if the engine broke down or blew up, or ran out of coal? So the first steamships still had sails.

However, as iron ships replaced wooden ships, steam engines really came into their own. They were used to drive screws (propellers), an improvement on paddles. Steamships crossed the Atlantic Ocean, proving that they were just as safe as sailing ships. And they were faster and kept better time, because they did not need to rely on the wind.

Above: Fulton's *Clermont* was the world's first practical steamboat. It carried passengers up the Hudson River from New York to Albany at almost 8 km/h. Its engine was built in England by Boulton and Watt, and drove two side paddle wheels.

Below: In April 1838 the steamships *Sirius* and *Great Western* raced each other across the Atlantic. *Sirius* was the first to reach New York. The larger *Great Western* steamed in only four hours behind, although she had started four days later. Designed by Isambard Kingdom Brunel, *Great Western* made the crossing in 15 days, half the time taken by a sailing ship.

For the glory of the fastest Atlantic crossing, liners steamed at full speed by day and night. In 1912 the world's largest liner, the *Titanic*, struck an iceberg during her maiden voyage. The 'unsinkable' ship sank with the loss of 1513 lives.

The first of the successful Stanley steam cars, 1899.

Steam on the Road

For hundreds of years inventors had dreamed of building machines which could move under their own power. But until the coming of the steam engine, none of these dreams had ever come true.

At last, in the 1800s, the 'horse-less carriage' arrived. Richard Trevithick's steam road carriages showed the way. But the clanking, puffing machines frightened horses and people so much that at first no one could see any use for them.

However, as better roads were made, steam coaches were tried out. They worked well but could not compete with horse-drawn coaches and the new railways.

A few rich people bought steam cars. The man whose job it was to stoke the fire was called the

Richard Trevithick built his first steam carriage in 1801. He drove it round his village in Cornwall and later took it to London. People were amazed to see it move without the aid of man or horse. By using high-pressure steam, Trevithick built engines which were small and light enough to be fitted to 'horseless carriages'.

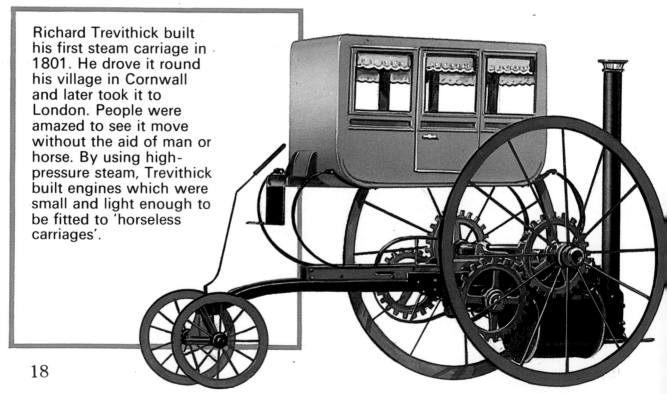

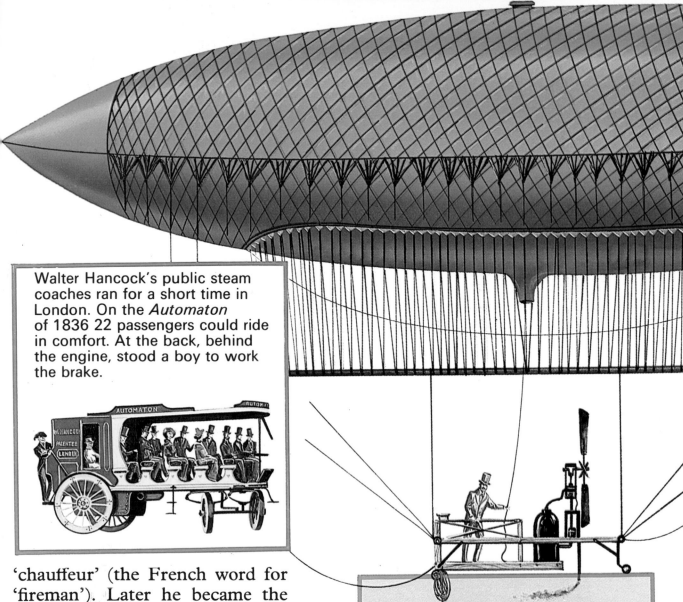

Walter Hancock's public steam coaches ran for a short time in London. On the *Automaton* of 1836 22 passengers could ride in comfort. At the back, behind the engine, stood a boy to work the brake.

'chauffeur' (the French word for 'fireman'). Later he became the driver. In front of the car walked another man with a red flag to warn other road-users of its approach.

In the 1880s steam cars became more popular. At the same time Karl Benz and Gottlieb Daimler were building the first cars with petrol engines. But for years steam cars were smoother to ride in, easier to drive and faster. In 1906 a Stanley steam car set a world speed record of 204 km/h.

STEAM IN THE AIR

By the 1800s balloons were quite common. But there was no way of steering a balloon, It floated whichever way the wind blew it. In 1852 the French engineer Henri Giffard built a cigar-shaped balloon and fitted a steam engine to the basket underneath. The engine drove a large propeller. This was the first airship. It could fly under its own power, provided there was little wind. But steam engines were really too heavy to be used in flying machines.

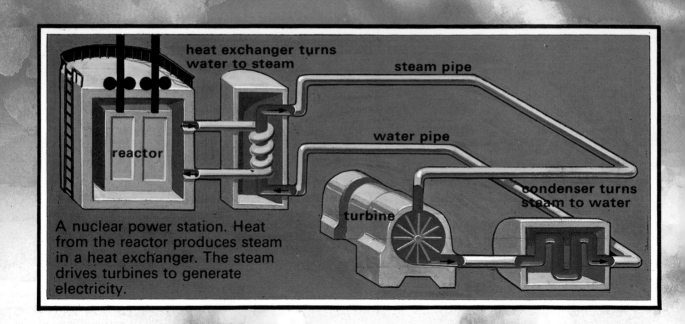

heat exchanger turns
water to steam

steam pipe

reactor

water pipe

condenser turns
steam to water

turbine

A nuclear power station. Heat
from the reactor produces steam
in a heat exchanger. The steam
drives turbines to generate
electricity.

A New Steam Age

We still live in the steam age today. Steam turbines are used to drive the engines of huge ships and to make electricity in power stations. In some ways, these steam engines have not changed very much since the great days of steam.

We also use steam in new ways. We live in the nuclear age. Atomic bombs are so terrible that one could destroy an entire city. But there are peaceful uses for this power. It can drive the engines of ships and submarines. And it can be used in power stations.

The 'reaction' inside a nuclear reactor produces enormously high temperatures. This heat is used to turn water into steam, and the steam drives turbines to make electricity. So the nuclear age is also the new steam age.

In some parts of the world hot springs, or geysers, and boiling mud bubble up from deep underground. This natural energy comes from layers of hot volcanic rock. It is called 'geothermal power'. 'Geothermal' means 'heat from the Earth'.

By drilling into the rock, the heat can be controlled and used to drive steam turbines. Electricity is made by geothermal power stations in Italy and New Zealand.

The steam age produced many curious machines. Some are pictured here.

1. John Ericsson's steam locomotive *Novelty* had an upright boiler. The train it is pulling includes flat wagons carrying the private coaches of rich passengers.

2. Morton's steam washing machine of 1884 was worked by turning a handle but was steam-heated.

3. The first steam-driven vehicle was Nicholas Cugnot's carriage. The boiler was so small that it only ran for 15 minutes.

4. Even odder was David Gordon's steam vehicle, which had moving 'legs' to help push it along.

5. A gentleman's steam carriage of 1884, before petrol-engined cars had replaced steam.

6. In 1805 Oliver Evans built this steam-driven dock-cleaning barge. Fitted with wheels, it ran on land for a short while.

7. The bat-like *Eole* was a steam-powered aeroplane built by Clement Ader. In 1890 it took off and made a short hop, but it could not fly properly.

7

6

5

Index

This revised expanded edition published in 1987 by Kingfisher Books Limited, Elsley Court, 20–22 Great Titchfield Street, London W1P 7AD
A Grisewood & Dempsey Company
Originally published in small format paperback by Pan Books Ltd in 1978.

© Grisewood & Dempsey Ltd 1978, 1987

Cover designed by The Pinpoint Design Company

BRITISH LIBRARY CATALOGUING IN PUBLICATION DATA
Rutland, Jonathan
    The age of steam. – rev. ed. –
    (Kingfisher explorer books)
    1. Steam-engines – History – Juvenile literature
    I. Title   II. Rutland, Jonathan, Exploring the age of steam
    621.1'09   TJ467

ISBN 0-86272-304-3

Phototypeset by Southern Positives & Negatives (SPAN), Lingfield, Surrey
Printed by Graficas Reunidas SA, Madrid, Spain